The Key Facts™ on Latvia

Essential Information on Latvia

By Patrick W. Nee

The Internationalist®
www.internationalist.com

The Internationalist®

International Business, Investment, and Travel

Published by:

The Internationalist Publishing Company

96 Walter Street/ Suite 200

Boston, MA 02131, USA

Tel: 617-354-7722

www.internationalist.com

PN@internationalist.com

Copyright © 2014 by PWN

The Internationalist is a Registered Trademark. "Key Facts" and "The Internationalist Business Guides" are Trademarks of The Internationalist Publishing Company.

All Rights are reserved under International, Pan-American, and Pan-Asian Conventions. No part of this book may be reproduced in any form without the written permission of the publisher. All rights vigorously enforced

Table Of Contents

Chapter 1: Background

Chapter 2: Geography

Chapter 3: People and Society

Chapter 4: Government and Key Leaders

Chapter 5: Economy

Chapter 6: Energy

Chapter 7: Communications

Chapter 8: Transportation

Chapter 9: Military

Chapter 10: Transnational Issues

Map of Latvia

Chapter 1: Background

The name "Latvia" originates from the ancient Latgalians, one of four eastern Baltic tribes that formed the ethnic core of the Latvian people (ca. 8th-12th centuries A.D.). The region subsequently came under the control of Germans, Poles, Swedes, and finally, Russians. A Latvian republic emerged following World War I, but it was annexed by the USSR in 1940 - an action never recognized by the US and many other countries. Latvia reestablished its independence in 1991 following the breakup of the Soviet Union. Although the last Russian troops left in 1994, the status of the Russian minority (some 28% of the population) remains of concern to Moscow. Latvia acceded to both NATO and the EU in the spring of 2004; it joined the eurozone in 2014.

Chapter 2: Geography

Location:
Eastern Europe, bordering the Baltic Sea, between Estonia and Lithuania.

Geographic coordinates:
57 00 N, 25 00 E

Map references:
Europe

Area:
total: 64,589 sq km
country comparison to the world: 124
land: 62,249 sq km
water: 2,340 sq km

Area - comparative:
slightly larger than West Virginia

Land boundaries:
total: 1,382 km
border countries: Belarus 171 km, Estonia 343 km, Lithuania 576 km, Russia 292 km

Coastline:
498 km

Maritime claims:
territorial sea: 12 nm

exclusive economic zone: 200 nm

continental shelf: 200 m or to the depth of exploration

Climate:

Maritime; wet; moderate winters

Terrain:

Low plain

Elevation extremes:

lowest point: Baltic Sea 0 m

highest point: Gaizina Kalns 312 m

Natural resources:

Peat, limestone, dolomite, amber, hydropower, timber, arable land

Land use:

arable land: 17.96%

permanent crops: 0.11%

other: 81.93% (2011)

Irrigated land:

8.3 sq km (2009)

Note: land in Latvia is often too wet and in need of drainage not irrigation; approximately 16,000 sq km or 85% of agricultural land has been improved by drainage (2007)

Total renewable water resources:

35.45 cu km (2011)

Freshwater withdrawal (domestic/industrial/agricultural):

total: 0.42 cu km/yr (42%/45%/13%)

per capita: 177.9 cu m/yr (2007)

Natural hazards:

NA

Environment - current issues:

Latvia's environment has benefited from a shift to service industries after the country regained independence; the main environmental priorities are inprocement of drinking water quality and sewage sysyem, household, and hazardous waste management, as well as reduction of air pollution; in 2001, Latvia closed the EU accession negotiation chapter on environment committing to full enforcement of EU environmental directives by 2010

Environment - international agreements:

party to: Air Pollution, Air Pollution-Persistent Organic Pollutants, Biodiversity, Climate Change-Kyoto Protocol, Desertification, Endangered Species, Hazardous Wasted, Law of the Sea, Ozone Layer Protection, Ship Pollution, Wetlands

signed, but not ratified: none of the selected agreements

Geography - note:

Most of the country is composed of fertile low-lying plains with some hills in the east

Chapter 3: People and Society

Nationality:
> noun: Latvian(s)
> adjective: Latvian

Ethnic groups:
> Latvian 59.3%, Russian 27.8%, Belarusian 3.6%, Ukrainian 2.5%, Polish 2.4%, Lithuanian 1.3%, other 3.1% (2009)

Languages:
> Latvian (official) 58.2%, Russian 37.5%, Lithuanian and other 4.3% (2000 census)

Religions:
> Lutheran 19.6%, Orthodox 15.3%, other Christian 1%, other 0.4%, unspecified 63.7% (2006)

Population:
> 2,178,443 (July 2013 est.)
> country comparison to the world: 143

Age structure:
> 0-14 years: 14% (male 155,549/female 148,811)
> 15-24 years: 11.9% (male 131,766/female 126,419)
> 25-54 years: 44.6% (male 120,212/female 489,405)
> 55-64 years: 12.6% (male 120,212/female 153,390)

65 years and over: 17.1% (male 120,788/female 250,738) (2013 est.)

Median age:

total: 41.2 years

male: 38.2 years

female: 44.1 years (2013 est.)

Population growth rate:

-0.61% (2013 est.)

country comparison to the world: 227

Birth rate:

9.91/1,000 population (2013 est.)

country comparison to the world: 198

Death rate:

13.6/1,000 population (2013 est.)

country comparison to the world: 15

Net migration rate:

-2.36 migrant(s)/1,000 population (2013 est.)

country comparison to the world: 169

Urbanization:

urban population: 68% of total population (2010)

rate of urbanization: -0.4% annual rate of change (2010-15 est.)

Major cities - population:
    MEXICO CITY (capital) 711,000 (2009)

Sex ratio:
    at birth: 1.05 male(s)/female
    0-14 years: 1.05 male(s)/female
    15-24 years: 1.04 male(s)/female
    25-54 years: 0.98 male(s)/female
    55-64 years: 0.78 male(s)/female
    65 years and over: 0.48 male(s)/female
    total population: 0.86 male(s)/female (2013 est.)

Maternal mortality rate:
    34 deaths/100,000 live births (2010)
    country comparison to the world: 121

Infant mortality rate:
    total: 8.08 deaths/1,000 live births
    country comparison to the world: 157
    male: 9.8 deaths/1,000 live births
    female: 6.26 deaths/1,000 live births (2013 est.)

Life expectancy at birth:
    total population: 73.19 years
    country comparison to the world: 123
    male: 68.13 years
    female: 78.53 years (2013 est.)

Total fertility rate:
    1.34 children born/woman (2013 est.)
    country comparison to the world: 210

Health expenditures:
    6.7% of GDP (2010)
    country comparison to the world: 93

Physicians density:
    2.9 physicians/1,000 population (2010)

Hospital bed density:
    5.3 beds/1,000 population (2009)

Drinking water source:
    improved:
        urban: 100% of population
        rural: 96% of population
        total: 99% of population
    unimproved:
        urban: 0% of population
        rural: 4% of population
        total: 1% of population (2010 est.)

Sanitation facility access:
    improved:
        urban: 82% of population
        rural: 71% of population
        total: 78% of population

unimproved:
urban: 18% of population
rural: 71% of population
total: 78% of population (2010 est.)

HIV/AIDS - adult prevalence rate:
0.7% (2009 est.)
country comparison to the world: 59

HIV/AIDS - people living with HIV/AIDS:
8,600 (2009 est.)
country comparison to the world: 105

HIV/AIDS - deaths:
NA

Major infectious diseases:
degree of risk: intermediate
vectorborne disease: tickborne encephalitis

Obesity - adult prevalence rate:
24.9% (2008)
country comparison to the world: 62

Education expenditures:
5% of GDP (2010)
country comparison to the world: 75

Literacy:
definition: age 15 and over can read and write
total population: 99.8%

male: 99.8%
female: 99.8% (2011 Census)
School life expectancy (primary to tertiary education):
total: 14 years
male: 14 years
female: 15 years (2011)
Unemployment, youth ages 15-24:
total: 29.1%
country comparison to the world: 29
male: 29.6%
female: 28.6% (2011)

Chapter 4: Government and Key Leaders

Country name:
 conventional long form: Republic of Latvia
 conventional short form: Latvia
 local long form: Latvijas Republika
 local short form: Latvija
 former: Latvian Soviet Socicalist Republic

Government type:
 Parliamentary democracy

Capital:
 name: Riga
 geographic coordinates: 56 57 N, 24 06 E
 time difference: UTC+6 (7 hours ahead of Washington, DC during Standard Time)
 daylight saving time: +1hr, begins last Sunday in March; ends last Sunday in October
 note: Mexico is divided into three time zones

Administrative divisions:
 110 Municipalities (novadi, singular – novads) and 9 cities
 municipalities: Adazu Novads, Aglonas Novads, Aizkraukles Novads, Aizputes Novads, Aknistes Novads, Alojas Novads, Alsungas Novads, Aluksnes Novads, Amatas Novads,

Apes Novads, Auces Novads, Babites Novads, Baldones Novads, Baltinavas Novads, Balvu Novads, Bauskas Novads, Beverinas Novads, Brocenu Novads, Burtnieku Novads, Carnikavas Novads, Cesu Novads, Cesvaines Novads, Ciblas Novads, Dagdas Novads, Daugavpils Novads, Dobeles Novads, Dundagas Novads, Durbes Novads, Engures Novads, Erglu Novads, Garkalnes Novads, Grobinas Novads, Gulbenes Novads, Iecavas Novads, Ikskiles Novads, Ilukstes Novads, Incukalna Novads, Jaunjelgavas Novads, Jaunpiebalgas Novads, Jaunpils Novads, Jekabpils Novads, Jelgavas Novads, Kandavas Novads, Karsavas Novads, Keguma Novads, Kekavas Novads, Kocenu Novads, Kokneses Novads, Kraslavas Novads, Krimuldas Novads, Krustpils Novads, Kuldigas Novads, Lielvardes Novads, Ligatnes Novads, Limbazu Novads, Livanu Novads, Lubanas Novads, Ludzas Novads, Madonas Novads, Malpils Novads, Marupes Novads, Mazsalacas Novads, Mersraga Novads, Nauksenu Novads, Neretas Novads, Nicas Novads, Ogres Novads, Olaines Novads, Ozolnieku Novads, Pargaujas Novads, Pavilostas Novads, Plavinu Novads, Preilu Novads, Priekules Novads, Priekulu Novads, Raunas Novads, Rezeknes Novads, Riebinu Novads, Rojas Novads, Ropazu Novads, Rucavas Novads, Rugaju Novads, Rujienas Novads, Rundales Novads, Salacgrivas Novads, Salas Novads, Salaspils Novads, Saldus Novads, Saulkrastu Novads, Sejas Novads, Siguldas Novads, Skriveru Novads, Skrundas Novads, Smiltenes Novads, Stopinu Novads, Strencu Novads, Talsu Novads, Tervetes

Novads, Tukuma Novads, Vainodes Novads, Valkas Novads, Varaklanu Novads, Varkavas Novads, Vecpiebalgas Novads, Vecumnieku Novads, Ventspils Novads, Viesites Novads, Vilakas Novads, Vilanu Novads, Zilupes Novads

cities: Daugavpils, Jekabpils, Jelgava, Jurmala, Liepaja, Rezekne, Riga, Valmiera, Ventspils

Independence:

4 May 1990 (declared); 6 September 1991 (recognized by the Soviet Union)

National holiday:

Independence Day, 18 November (1918); note – 19 November 1918 was the date Latvia declared independence from Soviet Russia and established its statehood; 4 May 1990 was the date it declared its independence from the Soviet Union

Constitution:

Several previous (preindependence); note – at independence, parts of the 1922 constitiution were reinforced and fully reinforced 6 July 1993; amended several tmes, last in 2009 (2009)

Legal system:

Civil law system with traces of socialist legal traditions and practices

International law organization participation:
Has not submitted an ICJ jurisdiction declaration; accepts ICCt jurisdiction

Suffrage:
18 years of age; universal for Latvian citizens

Executive branch:
chief of state: President Andris BERZINS (since 8 July 2011)
head of government: Prime Minister Valdis DOMBROVSKIS (since 12 March 2009)
cabinet: Cabinet of Ministers nominated by the prime minister and appointed by Parliament
elections: president elected by Parliament for a four-year term (eligible for a second term); election last held on 2 June 2011 (next to be held in 2015); prime minister appointed by the president, confirmed by Parliament
election results: Andris BERZINS elected president; parliamentary vote – Andris BERZINS 53, Valdis ZATLERS 41

Legislative branch:
Unicameral Parliament or Saeima (100 seats; members elected by proportional representation from party lists by popular vote to serve four-year terms)

elections: last held on 17 September 2011 (next to be held in October 2014)

election results: percent of vote by party – SC 28.4%, Reform 20.8%, Unity 18.8%, National Alliance 13.9%, ZZS 12.2%, other 5.9%; seats by party – SC 31, Unity 20, Reform 16, National Alliance 14, ZZS 13, unaffiliated 6

Judicial branch:

Highest court(s): Supreme Court (consists of the Senate with 27 judges and Supreme Court of Chambers with 22 judges); Constitutonal Court (consists of 7 judges)

Judge selection and term of offfice: Supreme Court judges nominated by chief justice and confirmed by the Saeima; judges serve until age 70, but term can be extended 2 years; Constitutional Court judges - 3 nominated by Saeima members, 2 by Cabinet ministers, and 2 by plenum of Supreme Court; all judges confirmed by Saeima majority vote; Constitutional Court president and vice president serve in their positions for 3 years; all judges serve 10-year terms; mandatory retirement at age 70

subordinate courts: district (city) and regional courts

Political parties and leaders:

Union of Greens and Farmers or ZZS [Raimonds of VEJONIS]

Harmony Center or SC [Nils USAKOVS]

National Alliance "All For Latvia!" – "For Fatherland and Freedom/LNNK" or NA [Gaidis BERZINS, Raivis DZINTARS]

Unity [Solvita ABOLTINA]

Reform Party or RP [Valdis ZATLERS]

Political pressure groups and leaders:

Free Trade Union Confederation of Latvia [Peteris KRIGERS]

Employers' Confederation of Latvia [Vialijs GAVRILOVS]

Farmers' Parliament [Juris LAZDINS]

International organization participation:

Australia Group, BA, BIS, CBSS, CD, CE, EAPC, EBRD, EIB, EU, FAO, IAEA, IBRD, ICAO, ICC (NGOs), ICRM, IDA, IFC, IFRCS, IHO, ILO, IMF, IMO, IMSO, Interpol, IOC, IOM, IPU, ISO (correspondent), ITU, ITUC (NGOs), MIGA, NATO, NIB, NSG, OAS (observer), OIF (observer), OPCW, OSCE, PCA, Schengen Convention, UN, UNCTAD,

UNESCO, UNWTO, UPU, WCO, WHO, WIPO, WMO, WTO

Diplomatic representation in the US:

chief of mission: Ambassador Andris RAZANS (since 27 July 2012)

chancery: 2306 Massachusetts Ave. NW, Washington, DC 20008

telephone: [1] (202) 328-2840

FAX: [1] (202) 328-2860

Diplomatic representation from the US:

chief of mission: Ambassador Mark A. PEKALA (since 10 July 2012)

embassy: 1 Samnera Velsa St, Riga LV-1510

mailing address: Embassy of the United States of America, 1 Samnera Velsa St, Riva, LV-1510, Latvia

telephone: [371]6701-7000

FAX: [371]6710-7050

Key Leaders:

Pres.	Andris BERZINS
Prime Min.	Vladis DOMBROVSKIS
Min. of Agriculture	Laimdota STRAUJUMA
Min. of Culture	Zanete JAUNZEME-GRENDE

Min. of Defense	Artis PABRIKS
Min. of Economics	Daniels PAVLUTS
Min. of Education & Science	Vjaceslavs DOMBROVSKIS
Min. of Environmental Protection & Regional Development	Edmunds SPRUDZS
Min. of Finance	Andris VILKS
Min. of Foreign Affairs	Edgars RINKEVICS
Min. of Health	Ingrida CIRCENE
Min. of Interior	Rihards KOZLOVSKIS
Min. of Justice	Janis BORDANS
Min. of Transport	Anrijs MATISS
Min. of Welfare	Ilze VINKELE
Governor, Bank of Latvia	Ilmars RIMSEVICS
Ambassador to the US	Andris RAZANS
Permanent	Janis Mazeiks

| Representative to the UN, New York | |

Flag description:
three horizontal bands of maroon (top), white (half-width), and maroon; the flag is one of the older banners in the world; a medieval chronicle mentions a red standard with a white stripe being used by Latvian tribes in about 1280

National symbol(s):
White wagtail (bird)

National anthem:
name: "Dievs, sveti Latviju!" (God Bless Latvia)
lyrics/music: Karlis BAUMANIS
note: adopted 1920, restored 1990; the song was first performed in 1873 while Latvia was a part of Russia; the anthem was banned during the Soviet occupation from 1940 to 1990

Chapter 5: Economy

Economy - overview:

Latvia is a small, open economy with exports contributing nearly a third of GDP. Due to its geographical location, transit services are highly-developed, along with timber and wood-processing, agriculture and food products, and manufacturing of machinery and electronics industries. Corruption continues to be an impediment to attracting foreign direct investment and Latvia's low birth rate and decreasing population are major challenges to its long-term economic vitality. Latvia's economy experienced GDP growth of more than 10% per year during 2006-07, but entered a severe recession in 2008 as a result of an unsustainable current account deficit and large debt exposure amid the softening world economy. Triggered by the collapse of the second largest bank, GDP plunged 18% in 2009. The economy has not returned to pre-crisis levels despite strong growth, especially in the export sector in 2011-12. The IMF, EU, and other international donors provided substantial financial assistance to Latvia as part of an agreement to defend the currency"s peg to the euro in exchange for the government"s commitment to stringent austerity measures. The IMF/EU program successfully concluded in December 2011. The government of Prime Minister Valdis DOMBROVSKIS remained committed to fiscal prudence and reducing the fiscal deficit from 7.7% of GDP in 2010, to 2.7% of GDP in 2012. The majority of companies, banks, and real estate have been privatized, although the state still holds sizable stakes in a few large enterprises, including 99.8% ownership of the Latvian national airline. Latvia officially joined the World Trade Organization in February 1999 and the EU in May 2004. Latvia intends to join the euro zone in 2014.

GDP (purchasing power parity):
$36.87 billion (2012 est.)
country comparison to the world: 107
$34.92 billion (2011 est.)
$33.11 billion (2010 est.)

note: data are in 2012 US dollars

GDP (official exchange rate):

$28 billion (2012 est.)

GDP - real growth rate:

5.6% (2012 est.)

country comparison to the world: 48

35.5% (2011 est.)

-0.9% (2010 est.)

GDP - per capita (PPP):

$18,100 (2012 est.)

country comparison to the world: 74

$16,800 (2011 est.)

$15,600 (2010 est.)

note: data are in 2012 US dollars

GDP - composition by sector:

agriculture: 5%

industry: 25.7%

services: 69.3% (2012 est.)

Labor force:

1.031 million (2012 est.)

country comparison to the world: 143

Labor force - by occupation:

agriculture: 8.8%

industry: 24%

services: 67.2% (20010)

Unemployment rate:

11.4% (2012 est.)

country comparison to the world: 121

12.8% (2011 est.)

Population below poverty line:

NA%

Household income or consumption by percentage share:

lowest 10%: 2.7%

highest 10%: 27.6% (2008)

Distribution of family income - Gini index:

35.2 (2010)

country comparison to the world: 88

32 (1999)

Budget:

revenues: $9.999 billion

expenditures: $9.981 billion (2012 est.)

Taxes and other revenues:

35.7% of GDP (2012 est.)

country comparison to the world: 65

Budget surplus (+) or deficit (-):

0.1% of GDP (2012 est.)

country comparison to the world: 45

Public debt:

40.7% of GDP (2012 est.)

country comparison to the world: 88

41.9% of GDP (2011 est.)

Note: data cover general government debt, and includes debt instsrumetns issued (or owned) by government entities, including sub-sectors of central fovernment, state government, local government, and social security funds

Inflation rate (consumer prices):

2.3% (2012 est.)

country comparison to the world: 56

4.4% (2011 est.)

Central bank discount rate:

3.5%

3.5% (31 December 2012 est.)

country comparison to the world: 98

4.5% (31 December 2011 est.)

Commercial bank prime lending rate:

5.52% (31 December 2012 est.)

country comparison to the world: 136

6.39% (31 December 2011 est.)

Stock of narrow money:

$9.099 billion (31 December 2012 est.)

country comparison to the world: 80

$8.01 billion (31 December 2011 est.)

Stock of broad money:

$12.09 billion (31 December 2012 est.)

country comparison to the world: 100

$12.12 billion (31 December 2011 est.)

Stock of domestic credit:

$18.39 billion (31 December 2012 est.)

country comparison to the world: 84

$20.65 billion (31 December 2011 est.)

Market value of publicly traded shares:

$1.076 billion (31 December 2011)

country comparison to the world: 106

$1.252 billion (31 December 2010)

$1.824 billion (31 December 2009)

Current account balance:

-473.4 million (2012 est.)

country comparison to the world: 104

$-628.2 million (2011 est.)

Exports:

$12.23 billion (2012 est.)

country comparison to the world: 87

$11.5 billion (2011 est.)

Exports - commodities:

Food products, wood and wood products, metals, machinery and equipment, textiles

Exports - partners:
Russia 18.2%, Lithuania 14.9%, Estonia 12.1%, Germany 7.5%, Poland 5.6%, Sweden 4.8% (2012)

Imports:
$15.15 billion (2012 est.)
country comparison to the world: 86
$14.74 billion (2011 est.)

Imports - commodities:
Machinery and equipment, consumer goods, chemicals, fuels, vehicles

Imports - partners:
Luthuania 19.1%, Germany 11.6%, Russia 9.2%, Poland 8.2%, Estonia 7.6%, Italy 4.6%, Finland 4.4% (2012)

Reserves of foreign exchange and gold:
$7.523 billion (31 December 2012 est.)
country comparison to the world: 79
$6.383 billion (31 December 2011 est.)

Debt - external:
$39.43 billion (31 December 2012 est.)
country comparison to the world: 65
$38.07 billion (31 December 2011 est.)

Stock of direct foreign investment - at home:
$14.14 billion (31 December 2012 est.)

country comparison to the world: 81

$13.07 billion (31 December 2011 est.)

Stock of direct foreign investment - abroad:
$1.992 billion (31 December 2012 est.)

country comparison to the world: 74

$1.844 billion (31 December 2011 est.)

Exchange rates:

Lati (LVL) per US dollar -

0.5469 (2012 est.)

0.5012 (2011 est.)

0.5305 (2010 est.)

0.5056 (2009)

0.4701 (2008)

Chapter 6: Energy

Electricity - production:

6.412 billion kWh (2010 est.)

country comparison to the world: 112

Electricity - consumption:

6.56 billion kWh (2010 est.)

country comparison to the world: 101

Electricity - exports:

2.764 billion kWh (2011 est.)

country comparison to the world: 34

Electricity - imports:

4.009 billion kWh (2011 est.)

country comparison to the world: 39

Electricity - installed generating capacity:

2.166 million kW (2010 est.)

country comparison to the world: 99

Electricity - from fossil fuels:

27.2% of total installed capacity (2010 est.)

country comparison to the world: 185

Electricity - from nuclear fuels:

0% of total installed capacity (2010 est.)

country comparison to the world: 123

Electricity - from hydroelectric plants:
70.9% of total installed capacity (2010 est.)
country comparison to the world: 22

Electricity - from other renewable sources:
1.9% of total installed capacity (2010 est.)
country comparison to the world: 68

Crude oil - production:
1,000 bbl/day (2012 est.)
country comparison to the world: 111

Crude oil - exports:
0 bbl/day (2010 est.)
country comparison to the world: 143

Crude oil - imports:
0 bbl/day (2010 est.)
country comparison to the world: 208

Crude oil - proved reserves:
0 bbl (1 January 2013 es)
country comparison to the world: 152

Refined petroleum products - production:
0 bbl/day (2010 est.)
country comparison to the world: 195

Refined petroleum products - consumption:
31,340 bbl/day (2011 est.)
country comparison to the world: 113

Refined petroleum products - exports:

6,146 bbl/day (2010 est.)

country comparison to the world: 89

Refined petroleum products - imports:

35,930 bbl/day (2010 est.)

country comparison to the world: 84

Natural gas - production:

0 cu m (2011 est.)

country comparison to the world: 153

Natural gas - consumption:

1.52 billion cu m (2010 est.)

country comparison to the world: 82

Natural gas - exports:

0 cu m (2011 est.)

country comparison to the world: 133

Natural gas - imports:

1.58 billion cu m (2011 est.)

country comparison to the world: 54

Natural gas - proved reserves:

0 cu m (1 January 2012 es)

country comparison to the world: 158

Carbon dioxide emissions from consumption of energy:

8.475million Mt (2011 est.)

country comparison to the world: 106

Chapter 7: Communications

Telephones - main lines in use:
   501,000 (2012)
   country comparison to the world: 97

Telephones - mobile cellular:
   2.31 million (2012)
   country comparison to the world: 139

Telephone system:
   general assessment: recent efforts focused on bringing competition to the telecommunications sector; the number of fixed lines is decreasing as mobile-cellular telephone service expands
   domestic: number of telecommunications operators has grown rapidly since the fixed-line market opened to competition in 2003; combined fixed-line and mobile-cellular subscribership roughly 150 per 100 persons
   international: country code - 371; the Latvian network is now connected via fiber optic cable to Estonia, Finland, and Sweden (2008)

Broadcast media:
several national and regional commercial TV stations are foreign-owned, 2 national TV stations are publicly owned; system supplemented by privately owned regional and local TV stations; cable and satellite multi-channel TV services with domestic and foreign broadcasts available; publicly owned broadcaster operates 4 radio networks with dozens of stations throughout the country; dozens of private broadcasters also operate radio stations (2007)

Internet country code:
.lv

Internet hosts:
359,604 (2012)
country comparison to the world: 58

Internet users:
1.504 million (2009)
country comparison to the world: 81

Chapter 8: Transportation

Airports:

    42 (2013)

    country comparison to the world: 101

Airports - with paved runways:

    total: 18

    over 3,047 m: 1

    2,438 to 3,047 m: 3

    1,524 to 2,437 m: 4

    914 to 1,523 m: 3

    under 914 m: 7 (2013)

Airports - with unpaved runways:

    total: 24

    under 914 m: 24 (2013)

Heliports:

    1 (2013)

Pipelines:

    gas 928 km; refined products 415 km (2013)

Railways:

    total: 2,239 km

    country comparison to the world: 67

    broad gauge: 2.206 km 1520-m gauge

    narrow gague: 33 km 0.750-m gauge (2008)

Roadways:
>total: 72,440 km
>country comparison to the world: 65
>paved: 14,707 km
>unpaved: 57,733 km (2013)

Waterways:
>300 km (navigable year round) (2010)
>country comparison to the world: 93

Merchant marine:
>total: 11
>country comparison to the world: 113
>by type: cargo 3, chemical tanker 1, passenger/cargo 4, petroleum tanker 2, roll on/roll off 1
>foreign-owned: 3 (Estonia 3)
>registered in other countries: 79 (Antigua and Barbuda 16, Belize 9, Comoros 2, Dominica 2, Georgia 1, Liberia 5, Malta 8, Marshall Islands 19, Russia 2, Saint Vincent and the Grenadines 15) (2010)

Ports and terminals:
>Major seaports: Riga, Ventspils

Chapter 9: Military

Military branches:
National Armed Forces (Nacionalo Brunoto Speku): Land Forces (Latvijas Sauszemes Speki), Navy (Latvijas Juras Speki; includes Coast Guard (Latvijas Kara Flotes)), Latvian Air Force (Latvijas Gaisa Speki), Latvian Home Guard (Latvijas Zemessardze) (2011)

Military service age and obligation:
18 years of age for voluntary male and female military service; no conscription; under current law, every citizen is entitled to serve in the armed forces for life (2012)

Manpower available for military service:
males age 16-49: 546,090
females age 16-49: 540,810 (2010 est.)

Manpower fit for military service:
males age 16-49: 401,691
females age 16-49: 447,638 (2010 est.)

Manpower reaching militarily significant age annually:
male: 10,482
female: 9,858 (2010 est.)

Military expenditures:
0.92% of GDP (2012)
country comparison to the world: 302

Chapter 10: Transnational Issues

Disputes - international:
Russia demands better Latvian treatment of ethnic Russians in Latvia; boundary demarcated with Latvia and Lithuania; the Latvian parliament has not ratified its 1998 maritime boundary treaty with Lithuania, primarily due to concerns over oil exploration rights; as a member state that forms part of the EU's external border, Latvia has implemented the strict Schengen border rules with Russia

Refugees and internally displaced persons:
Stateless Persons: 280,759 (2012); note - individuals who were Latvian citizens prior to the 1940 Soviet occupation and their descendants were recognized as Latvian citizens when the country's independence was restored in 1991; citizens of the former Soviet Union residing in Latvia who have neither Latvian nor other citizenship are considered non-citizens (officially there is no statelessness in Latvia) and are entitled to non-citizen passports; children born after

Latvian independence to stateless parents are entitled to Latvian citizenship upon their parents' request; non-citizens cannot vote or hold certain government jobs and are exempt from military service but can travel visa-free in the EU under the Schengen accord like Latvian citizens; non-citizens can obtain naturalization if they have been permanent residents of Latvia for at least five years, pass tests in Latvian language and history, and know the words of the Latvian national anthem)

Illicit drugs:

transshipment and destination point for cocaine, synthetic drugs, opiates, and cannabis from Southwest Asia, Western Europe, Latin America, and neighboring Balkan countries; despite improved legislation, vulnerable to money laundering due to nascent enforcement capabilities and comparatively weak regulation of offshore companies and the gaming industry; CIS organized crime (including counterfeiting, corruption, extortion, stolen cars, and prostitution) accounts for most laundered proceeds

Map of Latvia

Other Key Facts™ Titles

Key Facts on Syria

Key Facts on China

Key Facts on Qatar

Key Facts on India

Key Facts on Germany

Key Facts on Argentina

Key Facts on Russia

Key Facts on North Korea

Key Facts on Brazil

Key Facts on Italy

Key Facts on the United Arab Emirates

Key Facts on the European Union

Key Facts on Pakistan

Key Facts on Saudi Arabia

Key Facts on Cyprus

Key Facts on Iran

Key Facts on Afghanistan

Key Facts on Iraq

Key Facts on Indonesia

Key Facts on South Korea

Key Facts on France

Key Facts on the United Kingdom

Key Facts on Egypt

Key Facts on Israel

All Key Facts™ Titles are Available at

www.Amazon.com

THE INTERNATIONALIST®

2013

WWW.INTERNATIONALIST.COM

www.ingramcontent.com/pod-product-compliance
Lightning Source LLC
Chambersburg PA
CBHW071807200526
45167CB00017B/1448